TABLE OF CONTENTS

CHAPTER 1: INTRODUCTION

For anyone who thought the twenty first century would be one of reduced conflict and harmony, the evidence so far reflects that this century is just like any other in terms of conflict. The United States is in an unfamiliar situation as the lone super power without a significant existential threat. China is a rising power and Russia aspires to reclaim its role as a dominant player on the international stage. The U.S. position of world leadership, the country's prosperity and priceless freedoms, and the safety of the American people are challenged not only by a profusion of new and unpredictable threats, but also by the now undeniable fact that the national security system of the U.S. is increasingly misaligned with a rapidly changing global security environment.[1]

Over the past decade, the U.S. relied heavily on the military element of national power to influence the rest of the world. However, the global environment is changing rapidly, and the ways and means to influence it must keep up with the pace of change. If the U.S. is to continue to thrive in the twenty first century, it must adopt a national security structure capable of producing a strategy reflective of the changing environment where employment of the instruments of national power keeps pace with the changing security environment.

External or internal forces drive reform in the form of a champion. Historical examples such as the National Security Act of 1947 and the 1986 Goldwater Nichols Act demonstrate that reform championed by an external actor is more successful in achieving comprehensive and enduring changes making it the desired reform approach. Internal

---

[1] Project on National Security Refrom (PNSR), *Forging a New Shield,* (Washington DC: PNSR, November 2008), i.

champions of reform compete with organizational parochialism that produces barriers, which limit the extent of reform. Additionally, organizational authorities of the champion limit the internal champion's ability to influence reform outside of their direct responsibility, much like Secretary Elihiu Root's reform of the War Department in 1903 in which the Department of the Navy rebuked.

The United States current strategic environment is dominated by the fiscal environment and not ripe for an external champion for national security reform to evolve. During combat operations, the Department of Defense and whole of government under goes adaptation. As current operations wind down, the time is now to cement the lessons learned from over a decade at war. Due to the current strategic environment, internal reform is the most likely method to drive reform. The stimuli for reform in the national security structure often find their genesis in Department of Defense (DoD) reform efforts. History demonstrates that reform of the national security structure or DoD requires a political champion upon whose authorities determines the depth and breadth of reform. The current U.S. strategic environment is polluted with bipartisan politics hampering the emergence of an external champion for national security reform. Until the strategic environment improves, DoD must continue to lead reform efforts from within. DoD plays a critical role in shaping the changes needed for the U.S. to remain a relevant international leader in the twenty first century.

Diplomatic and military elements of national power form the foundation of U.S. policy dating from actions by the Second Continental Congress to create a national army in 1775. Not until after World War II have information and economics grown into more prominent and credible instruments of national power. Throughout history, the U.S. had traditionally relied on defense with a small professional army backed by citizen-soldiers and volunteers organized by state within a militia model. The U.S. used this structure for political and philosophical reasons, fearing the concentration of power and subsequent menace to liberty embodied in a large, professional force under only federal control.[2] So great was the fear of concentrated power among the Founding Fathers of the Constitution that they divided authority over the armed forces within their checks and balances system, making the President Commander in Chief, but giving Congress fiscal control and leaving the states primarily responsible for the militia. Prior to the 1890s when the U.S. military acquired credible power projection capability, diplomats had to exercise caution to ensure influential means of persuasion were credible. Beginning with power projection during the Spanish-American War in 1898, the military element of national power has grown in importance as a credible deterrent to compliment the diplomatic efforts. The armed forces have a significant influence on today's national security policy and structure giving diplomats credible means of deterrence.

As the U.S. military evolved, so did the nation's approach to national security. In many ways, military reform influenced or occurred in conjunction with national security reform. The military has always been at the core of national security and a look at the military organization today and its evolution provides insights into the current national security structure and its future direction.

The military element of national power resident in the DoD continues to be the dominate instrument of national power today and throughout the twenty first century and as such must lead security transformation. Over the past decade of continuous combat

---

[2] Mark A. Stoler, *George C. Marshall: Solider-Statesman of the American Century* (New York: Simon & Schuster Macmillan, 1989), 19.

operations, DoD made great strides in the area of joint operations and interagency coordination. However, these changes have yet to be cemented into the department's processes. The Defense Department must continue to look forward and develop new military processes and ways to influence the global environment efficiently, effectively, and decisively in support of U.S. national interests in conjunction with a whole-of-government approach. This institutional change is necessary to keep pace with the changing security environment and to spur national security structure reform. Recognizing when to institutionalize change is just as critical as the change itself.

The Environment and National Security

"We are operating more joint than we ever have before."
Gen Martin Dempsey, 18th Chairman of the Joint Chiefs of Staff

As the DoD resets into a fiscally constrained environment, a historical look at major defense policy changes indicate that the time is now to cement the recent advances in jointness and interagency cooperation into the national security structure and military establishment. Major policy changes such as the National Security Acts of 1947 and the Goldwater Nichols Act were required to break the bureaucratic parochialism and to establish an atmosphere of jointness within the DoD.

Advancements in military technology providing cross-domain capabilities allow military leaders the ability to coordinate capabilities across multiple domains, creating synergistic effects to win the nations conflicts. The current service organizational structure established before cross-domain capabilities existed resulted in organizations centered on the primary domain in which they operate. The U.S. military services clearly reflect this organization: Army (land), Navy (maritime) and Air Force (air & space). These organizations are very effective at increasing and capitalizing on the capabilities within service domains, but create challenges in creating synergy across both domains and services. Many of the capabilities enabling rapid cross-domain integration evolved in the latter half of the twentieth century and were implemented within the DoD only in the last twenty to thirty years.

The U.S. has recently been engaged in major combat operations for the longest consecutive time period in its history. During this period, combat operations covered the traditional spectrum of warfighting from force-on-force, counter insurgency, to nation building. A relatively new domain, cyber, played a major role in these operations. Additionally, great strides were made in interagency coordination and planning, and in joint operations. Similar to the drawdown after World War II and the Cold War, the U.S. finds itself resetting into an environment with fiscal challenges, a new significant warfighting domain (Air in WORLD WAR II, Cyber today) and the strategic lessons learned during the recent conflict not yet institutionalized.

The longer lessons learned remain unimplemented and/or adopted as policy, the harder it will become to do so. The economic challenges facing the U.S. today constitute a threat to our national security. These challenges will spur increased parochialism between military services and government departments as they justify their share of a shrinking budget. The historical record demonstrates that declining budgets lead to a degree of inter-service competition that threatens the very security of the U.S. The current amount of U.S. debt is unprecedented. The European nation of Greece, on the brink of economic collapse, is threatening the solidarity of the European Union. By comparison, the debt the U.S. holds is higher per captia than Greece.

"America's debt will be $16.8 trillion by the end of the calendar year, compared to $441 billion for Greece…that means U.S. debt is $53,400 for every man, woman, and child, compared to $39,400 for every man, woman, and child in Greece"
Senate Budget Committee[3]

The current fiscal environment effects all government department and agencies, but has the greatest security impact in the DoD. If any type of reform is to occur, it will impact today's environment of jointness and interagency cooperation. The war in Afghanistan is drawing down, in part because of current fiscal realities. The vicious interservice battles that took place after World War II reflect the effects of sharply reduced defense budgets.

History proves the only way to enact lasting reform is through legislation. The Goldwater-Nichols DoD Reform Act of 1986 is the last major legislation directing changes to DoD policy, operations and organization. It aimed to increase cooperation across the services and ensure seamless joint operations. Since that time, jointness has been an important consideration in the planning and funding of U.S. military forces.

Reform legislation achievement does not occur by happenstance. The military, in many ways is a reflection of society, just as the Founding Fathers of the Constitution designed. Congress has the responsibilities and authorities to manage the military. Therefore, military reform not representative of societal norms and current necessities has no chance for implementation.

The current Planning, Programming, Budgeting and Execution (PPBE) system is, in essence, about managing risk. However, reduced defense budgets pit the roles, missions, and associated programs of the services against each other. Declining defense

---

[3] U.S. Senate Committee on the Budget, "Charts," Republicans, http://budget.senate.gov/republican/public/index.cfm/charts (accessed December 3, 2012)

budgets will re-stoke the interservice budget and doctrine battles of the late 1940s.[4] The Defense Department's Air-Sea-Battle concept is sure to be a point of contention. Current and projected future cuts evoke parochialism within the DoD and the Navy views the refocus to the Pacific as a method to gain resources:

> *"if you look at the new strategy... it is a maritime-centric strategy"*
> Navy Secretary Ray Mabus comments at the Pentagon celebrating the Navy's 237th birthday[5]

Military Evolution

Joint Publication 1 defines joint as "activities, operations, and organization in which elements of two or more Military Departments participate."[6] The U.S. has been involved in joint activities since the Revolutionary War, but it is not until the Spanish American War in 1898 when joint became more than happenstance. Introduced in 1823, the Monroe Doctrine forced the military establishment to look at cross service coordination. The U.S. established the doctrine to prevent further colonization of North and South America by European nations and required a means to enforce it which did not come about until the 1890s.

The military needed to become a credible national instrument of power capable of force projection to enforce the Monroe Doctrine. Prior to 1898, most major conflicts occurred in North America (American Revolution, War of 1812, and Civil War) and did

---

[4] Mackubin Thomas Owens, "Declining Defense Budgets and the End of 'Jointness'," *National Review on Line*, July 27, 2012, under "Declining Defense Budgets and Jointness," http://www.nationalreview.com/articles/312312/declining-defense-budgets-and-end-jointness-mackubin-thomas-owens# (accessed October 10, 2012)

[5] Sydney J. Freedberg Jr, "On 237th Birthday, Navy Feels Its Time Has Come; Budget Pressures Belie Campaign Rhetoric," AOL Defense, http://defense.aol.com/2012/10/09/on-237th-birthday-navy-feels-its-time-has-come-budget-pressure/ (accessed December 3, 2012)

[6] U.S. Joint Chiefs of Staff, Doctrine for the Armed Forces of the U.S., Joint Publication 1 (Washington DC: Joint Chiefs of Staff, Incorporationg Change 1, March 20 2009), I-2.

not require comprehensive interservice coordination or cooperation. Since 1898, the national security interests of the U.S. require a military capability to project power outside of its borders, forcing the Army and Navy to work together in new ways. The first major test came during the Spanish American War when the U.S. challenged Spanish imperialism in the Far East and Latin America.[7] During this time period, the military establishment began to change its paradigm and seriously contemplate how each department could support the other.

Entering the twentieth century, the War Department and Navy Department recognized the need to operate and coordinate with each other. However, the services never fully embraced joint concepts and procedures, and used agreements and mutual cooperation as the premise to accomplish joint activities. This type of structure was representative of the existing national security organization. Two world wars, a depression, the emergence of the air domain, and the atomic era set the stage for the National Security Act of 1947. This Act was the first major defense reorganization legislation and established an organizational framework to promote jointness. The legislation attempted to establish conditions to supersede service agreements and allow for establishing joint doctrine, creating credible enduring joint principles, and empowering joint organizations. It would also provide an organization to assist the executive branch with interagency collaboration and coordination.

However, too much change too fast can actually be counterproductive, especially in large organizations. The National Security Act of 1947 established the DoD, the Air

---

[7] Graham A. Cosmas, *An Army for Empire; the U.S. Army in the Spanish-American War* (Columbia: University of Missouri Press, 1971), 35.

Force as a separate service, and established roles and missions for the services. These monumental changes resulted in a counterproductive joint effect as the Army and Navy fought to ensure their historic service equities remained intact. This led to parochialism as the Army and Navy entrenched and the Air Force fought to establish itself as equal to the other services. The framework created by the National Security Act of 1947 did not ensure jointness and an environment of service independence continued until 1986 and the Goldwater Nichols Act.

Following World War II, the U.S. became the preeminent free world power. The Cold War against the Soviet Union dominated the national security agenda for the next four decades. During this time, the national security organization became better equipped to coordinate a whole of government approach with the addition of the National Security Council and the placement of the military services under a Secretary of Defense. The reorganization legislations under Truman and Eisenhower took steps towards a unified national security structure, but it was unable to eliminate service parochialism and poor interagency coordination.

Containment policy was the driving force behind the nation's strategic security decisions during the cold war. A strong military, to serve as a major deterrent, was vital to ensuring success of the containment policy. However, the defense organization continued favoring service interests rather than the broader security interests of the nation.[8] The wars in Korea and Vietnam provided hope and evidence to the Soviet bloc that the U.S. could be defeated.

---

[8] James R. Locher, *Victory on the Potomac : The Goldwater-Nichols Act Unifies the Pentagon*, (College Station: Texas A & M University Press, 2002), 29. This is a summary of the author's view on DoD's priorities during the Cold War.

The whole-of-government approach to the cold war necessitated that each instrument of national power remained in equilibrium with one another. DoD's nuclear enterprise ensured the strategy of mutual assured destruction remained strong. However, U.S. military conventional operations underperformed producing small fissures in the containment policy. These weaknesses, if left unchecked, provided an area for the Soviet Union to exploit. The military's poor performance, primarily the result of poor joint integration in Operation Eagle Claw (Iranian Hostage Rescue), Operation Urgent Fury (Invasion of Grenada), combined with the bombing of the marine barracks in Beirut, Lebanon, provide the back drop and catalyst for the 1986 Goldwater Nichols Act.

The rate of change since Goldwater Nichols is on par with the strategic environmental change in the thirty-nine years between the 1947 NSA and Goldwater Nichols. The military received a much-needed overhaul with Goldwater Nichols, but the national security system is more than sixty years old and no longer helps American leaders to formulate coherent national strategy.[9] The national security structure has vertical cylinders of excellence, represented by the governmental departments, but little capability to coordinate and integrate horizontally. Today's threats are diverse, ambiguous, and express themselves in a multitude of potential forms that challenge the legacy national security system in use today.[10]

In order to understand the necessary changes needed to the national security structure and the mechanisms to do so, a look at back major military and national security changes and reforms enlightens, beginning with the Spanish-American War. Failure to

---

[9] Project on National Security Refrom (PNSR), *Forging a New Shield,* (Washington DC: PNSR, November 2008), i.

[10] Ibid., ii.

understand the ways and means to achieve necessary reform is critical, because American ingenuity cannot continue to be the basis for success. Rapidly changing security environments and multidimensional threats require a proactive approach to national security and a comprehensive security structure that supports a sound strategy by appropriating resources to support the national strategy versus department strategy.

CHAPTER 2: SPANISH AMERICAN WAR

The Spanish American War was a wakeup call for the U.S. military; joint military cooperation between the War and Navy Departments was essential to support the evolving national interests and policies. The Monroe Doctrine established in 1823 was the initial driving force.[1] This doctrine was the first significant U.S. policy requiring the military to plan for offensive operations (power projection) outside of its borders. Even though the doctrine was announced in 1823, the first real enforcement would not come until the Spanish American War in 1898. Early in the nineteenth century the U.S. was expanding westward in North America, under the dogma of Manifest Destiny. Later the country was drawn into depths of civil unrest leading to civil war from 1861-1865. Post-Civil and Indian wars, the military refocused on supporting the Monroe Doctrine. As America's place in and view of the world evolved, so did the thinking of its military leaders. Several significant military strategists from this period who outlined this new strategic view include Schofield, Mahan, and Upton.

The military establishment and particularly the authorities of the civilian and military leaders had yet to transform to the role and responsibilities we know today. Authority flowed from two distinct and antithetical chains of command. The first was the commanding general, who was responsible to the president for military operations. The second consisted of ten permanent bureau chiefs, who were responsible to the Secretary of War and the Congress. The 1895 Army Regulation defined the relationship between the two heads of the War Department in these words: "The military establishment is

---

[1] Department of State, Office of the Historian. "Milestones 1801-1829: Monroe Doctrine, 1823," Department of State, http://history.state.gov/milestones/1801-1829/Monroe (accessed November 10, 2012).

under the orders of the Commanding General of the Army in that which pertains to the discipline and military control. The fiscal affairs of the Army are conducted by the Secretary of War, through the several staff departments…All orders and instruction from the President or secretary of War, relating to military operations or affecting the military control and discipline of the Army, will be promulgated through the Commanding General."[2] This meant that the commanding general had no direct authority over the staff departments and his authority extended only to actual fighting units.

The secretaries of the services had the preponderance of power and often took control of the militaries, leaving the commanding general frustrated.[3] However, no law or regulation placed the Commanding General in a subordinate role to the Secretary and often personalities determined the role of the Commanding General. For instance, Ulysses S. Grant, while serving as the Commanding General, had a personal relationship with President Lincoln resulting in direct access to the Office of the President elevating the implied power for his position to almost an equal of the Secretary of War. This led to perceptions that while each Commanding General and Secretary acted on the Presidents orders, they did so independently of each other. However, over time, the Secretaries, as Presidential appointees, often held the upper hand and generally possessed greater power.

In practice, the Secretary of War controlled the Army, but often had no military experience and no body of military officers to offer advice. The issue was not that the Commanding General desired to avert the Secretary's authority, but the absence of an organizational structure to support each office and synchronize their activities and

---

[2] Graham A. Cosmas, *An Army for Empire; the U.S. Army in the Spanish-American War* (Columbia: University of Missouri Press, 1971), 20. The author is specifically referring to the War Department, however, the basic organizational structure and authorities for the Department of War and Department of Navy were similar. This reference is used to define what it was.
[3] Ibid., 21

policies. The result was organizational deficiencies and internal conflicts based on personalities and relationships to determine the depth of influence verses management based on statutory prescribed roles and responsibilities.

Bold Vision

Any organization not in sync with itself has a low probability of success. This was the state of the nation's military within the War Department and Navy Department during the 1800s. Personalities and relationships were dominate and defining factors behind the military instrument of power versus a coherent organizational structure and process.

The internal turmoil resulting from the department's organizational conflict and inefficiencies hampered any thought of jointness. Lieutenant General John M. Schofield's bold vision attempted to change this paradigm. Before becoming the Commanding General of the Army in 1888, Schofield held a variety of positions within the War Department. Awarded the Medal of Honor in 1862 for conspicuous gallantry during the battle of Wilson's Creek in Missouri, he commanded at all levels during the Civil War.[4] Following the Civil War, he served as the Secretary of War under President Andrew Johnson from June 1868 – March 1869 and Superintendent of the U.S. Military Academy from 1876 – 1881. He served seven years as the Commanding General of the Army before retiring in 1895 due to a mandatory retirement age of sixty-four. General Schofield had a unique and well-rounded background in both the political and military aspects of the Department equipping him with the knowledge and expertise to envision a new organizational philosophy and construct.

---

[4] Congressional Medal of Honor Society, "Recipients," Congressional Medal of Honor Society, http://www.cmohs.org/recipient-detail/1198/schofield-john-m.php (accessed 20 December 2012).

Lieutenant General Schofield brought three basic premises to the position of Commanding General: 1) the Army needed a single uniformed head, with power over the staff; 2) the Chain of command ran from the President to the Secretary of War with the Commanding General subordinate to the Secretary; 3) Commanding General's loyalty was to the position and not the administration.[5] Schofield envisioned an organizational structure closely aligned with contemporary Army organization design. He proposed a Chief of Staff versus a Commanding General with authority over the all the staff, but no authority to command. By clearly subordinating the Chief of Staff to the President and the Secretary, and by assuring political harmony with his superiors, Schofield sought to reinforce the authority of this officer over the rest of the Army, thus achieving the unity of control desired by the military reformers.[6]

During his tenure as Commanding General, Schofield was unable to persuade politicians to pass legislation that reflected his vision for military organizational reform. The argument to maintain the status quo in the late 1800s was that under the current system the nation had won all of its previous conflicts. Why change something that is successful? Despite this type of thinking, General Schofield put into practice his theories of command and established an environment which reduced organizational turmoil and facilitate cross service integration.[7] These were the first steps taken by the Army towards achieving real joint interaction between the services. Lieutenant General Schofield retired from the Army in 1895 and continued to perform an important advisory role until after the Spanish American War in 1898.

---

[5] Cosmas, *An Army for Empire; the U.S. Army in the Spanish-American War*, 28.
[6] Ibid., 29.
[7] John McAllister Schofield, *Forty-Six Years in the Army* (New York, The Century Company, 1897), 480.

Captain Alfred Thayer Mahan, a forward thinking naval officer, published a book in 1890, *The Influence of Sea Power Upon History*. It was one of the most influential books of its time and laid out a plan for American power based on a maritime strategy requiring the support of the War Department. The Monroe Doctrine and business interest aboard influenced his naval strategy. This strategy consisted of a fleet of ships and coaling stations to enforce/protect U.S. national interests abroad.

With this maritime focused strategy, the Navy took the leading role defending national interest abroad and the Army supported these efforts. A national military strategy to defend U.S. national interests began taking shape and the military departments seemed to be working together to support it. In 1897, retired Lieutenant General Schofield, summed up the Army's place in the new military posture: "In a country having the situation of the U.S., the navy is the aggressive arm of the national military power…one of the most important functions of the land defense: to give the aggressive arm secure bases of operation at all the great seaports where navy-yards or depots are located."[8]

The Army's responsibilities were primarily to protect the homeland and important outposts to help the Navy seize and hold strategic locations abroad. Hence, cooperation between the two services increased in strategy and supporting resource sharing. Additionally, the War Department embraced coastal defense as a core function well before the introduction of Mahan's maritime strategy. Budgets, reports and congressional testimony as early as 1885 reflected this strategic direction. Rebuilding the coastal defenses was expensive and slow. However, as conflict with Spain seemed more likely and Mahan's national maritime strategy came to fruition, the War Department

---

[8] Cosmas, *An Army for Empire; the U.S. Army in the Spanish-American War,* 38.

began to appropriate most of its budget to coastal defense, building a strategic shield to enable the Navy's mobility. As the U.S. began to embrace the requirements to support the Monroe Doctrine, the Department of the Navy was appropriated the majority of the national military budget. This is reflected in the 1898 defense appropriation, which provided the Department of the Navy $29 million and the War Department $19 million of which $15 million went towards coastal defense.[9]

A decade before Captain Alfred Thayer Mahan began promoting the new maritime strategy, Major General Emory Upton of the U.S. Army developed a plan well adapted to the requirements of modern tactics and maritime expansion.[10] In 1875-1876, sponsored by General Sherman and under War Department orders, Upton traveled around the world to study foreign militaries. He began in the East Pacific and worked his way westward. The Prussian military resonated with Upton and he based many of his arguments on lessons learned the from Franco-Prussian and Austro-Prussian wars. Among many of Upton's recommendations also supported by Schofield was the creation of a general staff. His report appeared in two influential books: *The Armies of Asia and Europe* and *The Military Policy of the U.S.*

Upton's influence was slow to gain acceptance and significant changes were slow in developing. General Sherman's comment on Upton's report, penciled on the cover, was that his ideas were sound, but: "I doubt if you will convince the powers that be . . . The time may not be now, but will come when these [conclusions] will be appreciated."[11]

---

[9] Ibid., 83.
[10] Ibid., 45.
[11] Adolf Carlson, *Joint U.S. Army-Navy War Planning on the Eve of the First World War: Its Origins and its Legacy*. Carlisle Barracks, PA: Strategic Studies Institute, February 16, 1998.

1898 and the Beginning of the Twentieth Century

With the U.S. Navy serving as the lead in a maritime focused strategy and war with Spain on the horizon, the Army saw a need for a larger strategic role including more resources. The Pacific was a region gaining the interest of a variety of nations as Germany was interested in expanding its influence in the region. The U.S. came into conflict with Germany in the Pacific fourteen years earlier in Samoa, as the U.S. attempted to block German expansionism.[12] President McKinley's orders necessitated an Army capable of establishing control of large landmasses, thousands of miles from the U.S. mainland, directed the War Department to prepare for invasion of Cuba and the Philippines. The U.S. Navy, under Admiral George Dewey, sailed into Manila Bay in May of 1898, effectively taking control of the Philippines from the Spanish. The Spanish were happy to let the U.S. have the Philippines and its growing insurgency.

The U.S. faced a dilemma; leave the Philippines unoccupied and exposed to German expansionism or confront the growing insurgency the Spanish had struggled to suppress. The U.S. decided in August 1898 to send 8,500 U.S. Army troops under the command of General Wesley Merritt to the Philippines to complete its conquest and pacification.[13] In reality, the U.S. took the Philippines from Spain and inherited an insurgency from the Spanish Army. Unlike the Cuban insurrectos, the Philippine insurgents had neither asked for nor welcomed U.S. assistance. The counterinsurgency went on intermittently from 1898 to 1913. For the first time in its history, the U.S. had to

---

[12] Ibid.
[13] Ibid.

maintain an army in a theater of war many thousands of miles away, underscoring the need for a close working relationship between the Navy and the Army.[14]

Despite military victories during the Spanish-American War, scandals tore the Army. The organization almost totally broke down under the strain of wartime mobilization and, in the process, revealed a host of serious problems. Troops destined for tropical Cuba arrived in Florida for embarkation with winter uniforms. Supplies were inadequate and ineffectively transported to the troops. Food turned out to be diseased. Transport to Cuba was insufficient, and no one seemed to possess an overall strategic plan or even basic knowledge of the enemy and the terrain the troops would be facing. Coordination between the Army and Navy in Cuba was abysmal, and the commanding officers of the two services seemed to spend more time fighting each other than the Spanish. U.S. soldiers and sailors performed well, but under such circumstances suffered high and unnecessary casualties. More of them fell to diseased meat and unsanitary living conditions than to Spanish bullets.[15]

The legacy of the War with Spain is mixed. For the Navy, the battles of Manila and Santiago Bay were legitimate victories but, for the Army, the victories resembled defeats. On the battlefields in Cuba, the U.S. Army was as valorous as ever, but for every American soldier killed by the enemy (381), more than four died due to the negligence or incompetence of the [War Department] (2061).[16]

The War Department received the majority of blame, particularly Secretary Russell Alger who was forced to resign in 1899. Reform was in order, and the instrument

---

[14] Ibid.

[15] Mark A. Stoler, *George C. Marshall: Solider-Statesman of the American Century* (New York: Simon & Schuster Macmillan, 1989), 18.

[16] Carlson, *Joint U.S. Army-Navy War Planning on the Eve of the First World War: Its Origins and its Legacy.*

of that reform was the newly appointed Secretary of War, Elihu Root. Root turned to

Schofield's philosophy and Upton's reports. Upton's incomplete manuscript remained

buried for over twenty years after his tragic suicide in 1881. Well known in army circles,

Secretary Root read and published Upton's reports when he took office.[17] Chief among

his recommendations included the institution of a general staff enacted in 1903 under the

General Staff Act and the creation of the "War Academy," implemented as the U.S.

Army War College in November 1904.[18] The Army and Navy finally possessed

complementary structures for the joint study of strategic problems. At the War College

dedication speech, Root encouraged the Army and Navy "never to forget your duty of

coordination . . . this is the time to learn to serve together without friction."[19] Schofield's

vision of a functioning joint staff would take over forty years to become a reality.

Elihu Root continued to capitalize on the progressive movement in the early

twentieth century by championing reform in the Department of State. After serving as

the Secretary of War, he became the Secretary of State from 1905-1909. He worked to

reorganize the Department of State in new and unprecedented ways. Root sought to

professionalize the Foreign Service and Consular Service, creating the first Foreign

Service Exam. He instituted new methods of record keeping in the Department, devised

a system of rotating members of the diplomatic service to give them a greater variety of

---

[17] Stoler, *George C. Marshall: Solider-Statesman of the American Century*, 20.
[18] Carlson, *Joint U.S. Army-Navy War Planning on the Eve of the First World War: Its Origins and its Legacy*.
[19] Ibid.

experience, and organized the Department by geographic regions.[20] These Departmental reforms ultimately proved more enduring than Root's contributions to foreign policy.[21]

The final ingredient in tying together the Army and Navy's efforts was the creation of the Joint Army and Navy Board in 1903, the first standing inter-service war planning committee in American history. The board consisted of four principal officers of each service whose function was to issue broad guidelines for the defense of the U.S., its possessions, and the Western Hemisphere. Detailed planning was the responsibility of the General Staff and the Navy Staffs, with most of the actual work done by the two war colleges.[22]

In response to a recommendation made by Army Chief of Staff Lieutenant General Adna R. Chaffee in April 1904, Secretary of War William Howard Taft directed the Joint Army-Navy Planning Board to identify and prioritize strategic challenges facing the U.S. potentially requiring joint Army Navy Action. Taft envisioned joint Army-Navy staff action during crisis execution.[23] The Joint Board's solutions to these "practical problems" would become war plans signed by the two service secretaries. This was the first joint deliberate planning system in American history.[24] Prior to 1919, the Joint Board lacked a working staff limiting the results from this initial joint planning and coordination effort.

The Joint Board possessed no real authority or power. The object of the Joint Board described in the directive of July 17, 1903 states: "[The Joint Army-Navy Board]

---

[20] Department of State, Office of the Historian, "Biographies of the Secretaries of State: Elihu Root." Department of State, http://history.state.gov/departmenthistory/people/root-elihu (accessed December 31, 2012).
[21] Ibid.
[22] Carlson, *Joint U.S. Army-Navy War Planning on the Eve of the First World War: Its Origins and its Legacy.*
[23] Ibid.
[24] Ibid.

to hold stated sessions and such extraordinary sessions as shall appear advisable for the purpose of conferring upon, discussion and reaching common conclusions regarding all matters calling for the cooperation of the two services."[25] The board was a formal body to address cooperation between the services but lacked any authority to require cooperation. The board had no permanent members and suffered the negative effects of service bias. Issues addressed by the board would often die when no common solutions could be agreed upon, which was often the case. The lack of authority and permanent members on the Joint Board limited its impact on cooperation between the Army and Navy. It was most effective when issues were equally beneficial to both services.

Analysis

In 1898, War and Navy Departments were unprepared for the strategic situation faced by the U.S. The U.S. was groping its way in the complicated game of international power and diplomacy, aware of its potential military strength and desirous of using it, but unsure exactly how to employ it for what specific purposes. The military failed to keep pace with the policies of the time. These policies reflected those of a mature, established state, while the military organization was still growing out of its infancy. The U.S. military was comfortable protecting and defending the homeland, and struggled to project power in support of a growing nation with international interests.

President McKinley's vacillating strategy and war aims, together with the fluctuating demands they imposed on the armed services, mirrored the larger national uncertainty.[26] The nation lacked a national security structure that combined all of the

---

[25] Joint Chiefs of Staff, Historical Division, *Origin of the Joint and Combined Chiefs of Staff, Volume I*, Vernon E. Davis, Joint Secretariat, (Washington DC, 1972), 6.

[26] Cosmas, *An Army for Empire; the U.S. Army in the Spanish-American War*, 313.

elements of national power to produce a comprehensive strategy needed to protect and advance national interests. Generals Schofield and Upton planted the seeds for military reform. Those seeds began to germinate when a flawed military doctrine effectively failed to support a national strategy. The War Department's inefficiency and incompetency in response to the conflicts in the Philippines and Cuba necessitated additional reform.

Prior to the twentieth century, the President as the Commander in Chief affected coordination between the War Department and Navy Department. Until the Spanish American War, all major coordinated efforts took place in North America and primarily at the tactical level. The military organizational structure did not facilitate operational and strategic interservice coordination. Army and Navy forces functioned autonomously with the President as their only common superior. This defunct interservice cooperation and lack of coordinated, joint military action had a negative impact on operations in the Philippines and Cuba during the Spanish-American War.

However, during this time, the services foreshadowed what joint cooperation was possible. The two military departments agreed and supported a common strategic doctrine. This was the first time senior service departmental level accomplished strategic coordination. The War Department also recognized its organizational deficiencies and followed Schofield's philosophy in creating a Chief of Staff. In reports after the Spanish-American War, the military departments acknowledge a failure to successfully plan and employ joint operations. This acknowledgment led to the creation of the Army-Navy Joint Board. The national security structure did not undergo a review. As the U.S. entered the twentieth century, it still lacked a process or organization to coordinate a whole-of-government approach to the nation's security interest outside of the President's cabinet.

While the two military departments strove to improve coordination with each other, the departments had different priorities and organizational cultures that limited the pace at which reform could occur. Lacking the pressures of the Army's wartime demands and failures, the Navy organizational reforms lagged far behind, despite determined efforts by reformers.[27] In 1900, responding to naval officers' pressures for a naval general staff to provide "central direction and control," the Navy secretary created the General Board, tasked merely with developing plans and furnishing advice. Navy Secretary Josephus Daniels "regarded a general staff not simply as unwise but as undemocratic and 'un-American.'"[28] This view continued to resonate inside the Navy through the post World War II era.

Upton and Schofield were unable to achieve the reforms they believed in because the services and country were not ready for such reforms. The catalyst for security reforms often comes at the expense of national security and the military. The Secretary of the Services, who are appointed by the President and served on his cabinet, was the authoritative voice for service organizations and hence the lowest level required to champion such reforms. Short of championing the changes oneself, documenting the rationale and reasons for change is critically important so that when the time is right for reform those ideas are not lost.

---

[27] James R. Locher, *Victory on the Potomac : The Goldwater-Nichols Act Unifies the Pentagon*, (College Station: Texas A & M University Press, 2002), 18.

[28] Ibid., 18.

The lessons learned from the Spanish-American War provided the catalyst for reform of the Army. Secretary of War, Elihu Root became the instrument of reform in 1903. American society was much more receptive to some of Upton's ideas than it had been earlier.[29] This was not simply because of the War Departments scandals during the Spanish-American War, but also because army reform fit in with the general reform movement sweeping the country.[30]

The U.S. was unwilling to enact any greater military reform during this time. It lacked the political will because there was not a large overt threat to the nation to create external pressures for reform. The global environment, societal norms and disparity between national instruments of power did not require significant interagency coordination to achieve national objectives. Just as the military departments were struggling coordinating with each other, so were the other government departments. This inevitably results in less than a coordinated whole-of-government approach to the nation's future conflicts. This framework guided the U.S. for another forty-plus years before another catalyst in concert with societal pressures changed the paradigm.

---

[29] Stoler, *George C. Marshall: Solider-Statesman of the American Century*, 20.
[30] Ibid., 20.

CHAPTER 3: NATIONAL SECURITY ACT OF 1947

JAPAN SURRENDERS, END OF WAR!
EMPEROR ACCEPTS ALLIED RULE
Headline, New York Times front page, August 14, 1945[1]

Four months later, President Harry Truman in his message to Congress on December 19, 1945, forcibly reminded lawmakers that when the U.S. entered World War II the national security structure was inadequate and there were two separate and independent departments of national defense, with no well-defined habits of coordination or cooperation. Nor was air power organized on an equal basis with the land and sea forces. A temporary war powers act served as an expedient tool in creating a joint chiefs of staff and other changes in the War and Navy Department. These improvisations contributed significantly to Allied success and may have spelled the difference between defeat and victory.[2] President Truman fully understood that unless Congress took further action within a limited time frame the national security structure and the military departments would revert to their prewar organizational status.

The U.S. entered World War II with a rudimentary national security structure. Only at the very top, the President, did responsibility over all aspects of national power consolidate in order to develop national strategy. In essence, national security policy rested with an individual versus an organizational structure that could shape and advise the executive branch. The formulation of sound national policies involved extended deliberations, taking into account a broad assessment of the country's capabilities and

---

[1] New York Times, "On This Day," New York Times on the Web, http://www.nytimes.com/learning/general/onthisday/20100814.html (accessed December 6, 2012).

[2] U.S. Air Force, Air University, *Unification of the Armed Forces: Administrative and Legislative Developments 1945-1949*, by R. Earl. McClendon. Documentary Research Division, Research Studies Institute. (Maxwell Air Force Base, Alabama, 1952).

vital interests. Nevertheless, in the U.S. governmental system prior to World War II, there had not developed any institution for the orderly and timely formulation of national policy, giving appropriate weight to its military, diplomatic, economic, and public and legislative aspects.[3]

The Depression following World War I overrode any appetite to make significant changes to the national or military structure or processes. Leading up to World War II, the War Department and Navy Department continued to act independently. The Joint Army-Navy Board, established in 1903, was still the main vehicle to facilitate coordination between the Chiefs of the two services. The board's early work focused on minor issues. During World War I, it virtually disappeared.[4] The two service secretaries attempted to strengthen the board after World War I. However, the two departments did not view it "as a means of drawing the two armed forces into ever closer integration."[5] The Army and Navy limited the board to "providing sufficient coordination to allow the two services to continue to operate autonomously in all major essentials."[6] This represented the extent of jointness in the military entering World War II.

President Roosevelt demonstrated the most telling evidence that the military organizational framework was inadequate in the summer of 1941, when he assumed the full authority of his constitutional role as Commander in Chief of the Armed Forces. Out of necessity, he worked to unify the military instrument of power. The War and Navy

---

[3] Joint Chiefs of Staff, Historical Division, *Origin of the Joint and Combined Chiefs of Staff, Volume I*, Vernon E. Davis, Joint Secretariat, (Washington DC, 1972), 32.

[4] James R. Locher, *Victory on the Potomac : The Goldwater-Nichols Act Unifies the Pentagon*, (College Station: Texas A & M University Press, 2002), 18.

[5] Joint Chiefs of Staff, Historical Division, *Origin of the Joint and Combined Chiefs of Staff, Volume I*, 28.

[6] Locher, *Victory on the Potomac*, 18.

Departments were virtually autonomous and incapable of harmonizing internal business activities and coordinating land, sea, and air operations.[7] The only direct and authoritative linking of the Army and Navy was through the person and power of the President as Commander in Chief, and in practice, this authority was exercised only in unusual cases.[8] As the rest of the world was drawn into World War II, the nation required coordination and responsive national security structure and the President, himself, acting as Commander in Chief, could only accomplish this.

The nation's security apparatus came under scrutiny on December 7, 1941. The Japanese surprise attack on Pearl Harbor exposed the weak national security structure and amplified the limitations with the concept of mutual cooperation between the military services. As John Gaddis observed, "surprise attacks tend to sweep away old conceptions of national security and what it takes to achieve it."[9] December 7th was more than just a day of infamy; it became the evidence and the catalyst required to overhaul the national security organization.

British Influence

Great Britain was at war with the Axis powers for two years and transformed its organizations and processes to reflect wartime needs. Prior to its declaration of war against Germany in September 1939, Britain debated consolidating its three services

---

[7] Ibid., 19.

[8] Joint Chiefs of Staff, Historical Division, *Origin of the Joint and Combined Chiefs of Staff, Volume I,* 27.

[9] John Lewis Gaddis, *Surprise, Security and the American Experience,* (Cambridge, Massachusetts: President and fellows of Harvard College, 2004), 37.

under a Ministry of Defence.[10] The debates that surrounded military reorganization in

Britain resonated ten years later on the other side of the Atlantic Ocean.

Paul Smith captured the debates in Britain and summed them up this way:

> While a Ministry of Defence was attractive in theory, as it would replace three conflicting Services with unified defence, no one was brave enough to try it in practice given Britain's political and constitutional circumstances. The Committee of Imperial Defence had obvious faults when it came to bringing the government and the Services closer together. It was a forum for talk rather than action, compromise rather than resolution. It compartmentalised and decentralised defence decision making and avoided controversial issues, while its lack of executive authority left the Service Departments to interpret its conclusions as they saw fit. The creation of the Chief of Staff only emphasised the separation of the military chiefs from civilian policy makers and financiers.[11]

The arguments used in Britain during the 1930s are almost identical to the ones

President Truman used in 1945 asking Congress to implement military reform. Before

World War II, Britain's Chief of Staff operated much like the Joint Army-Navy Board of

the U.S. December 16, 1935, in a letter to The Times newspaper in London, Hugh

Trenchard outlined the problems of coordination in the Chiefs of Staff in explicit detail.

He summarized it by pointing out the Chiefs of Staff worked by compromise rather than

co-operation, and it was time for a ministerial chairman with a permanent staff to oversee

rearmament.[12]

Reform is never easy; many variables require coordination for change to occur.

Even though Britain introduced the concepts of significant national security reform as

early as 1890, it took another world war and the advent of Winston Churchill before the

Great Britain took the first practical step towards unified defence administration. This

---

[10] Paul Smith, *Government and the Armed Froces in Britain*, 1856-1990 (London, GBR: Continuum International Publishing), 1996, 153.

[11] Paul Smith, *Government and the Armed Froces in Britain*, 153.
[12] Ibid., 148.

was required for many of the same reasons that President Roosevelt fulfilled his constitutional authorities as Commander in Chief. Not until 1964 would Great Britain create the Ministry of Defence. From its conception in 1890 it took seventy-four years for a Ministry of Defence to géstate, a long time even in Britain's traditionally lethargic political system.[13]

By the time the U.S. entered the War, the British refined their joint organizational structure and processes to reflect a streamlined system and processes to unifying the military instrument of power. After the attack on Pearl Harbor, senior leaders in the U.S. realized a more ambitious and coherent arrangement was required to assist the president in the formulation of military policies. During the Arcadia Conference (December 22, 1941, to January 14 1942) between Churchill, Roosevelt, and respective military advisers, the American service chiefs realized that the British Chiefs of Staff enjoyed a considerable advantage in negotiations because they frequently presented a common front on issues of strategy.[14] U.S. senior leaders determined the need to formulate a body comparable to the British Chiefs of Staff to communicate more effectively with their British counterparts. They created the Joint Chiefs of Staff (JCS) to include the means capable of unified command for all of the armed forces.

The newly created Joint Chiefs of Staff effectively replaced the Army-Navy Joint Board. One of the main differences between the two was the elevation of the Chief of Staff of the Army Air Forces to a co-equal with the Chief of Staff of the Army and the Chief of Naval Operations.[15] Britain established their air arm as a separate service in

---

[13] Ibid., 153.

[14] Douglas T. Stuart, *Creating the National Security State* (New Jersey: Princeton University Press, 2008), 52.

[15] Ibid., 52.

1918; the Americans required a counterpart with equal authority to ensure effective negotiations.

As the war progressed, senior military officers recognized a change in civil-military relations. President Roosevelt relied heavily on the Joint Chiefs of Staff for more than just military advice and the Joint Chiefs became accustomed to and protective of their privileged position in Washington.[16] Military leaders like General Marshall recognized that the civil-military situation had the potential to develop into something counterproductive. Marshall and the other members of the Joint Chiefs of Staff were introduced to a very different, and frequently more effective, model of civilian-military cooperation in their routine interactions with their British counterparts.[17] The skill and ease with which British representatives utilized their War Cabinet to reconcile the demands of diplomacy and war fighting was not lost on thoughtful American policymakers.[18]

Interagency Cooperation

As the end of the war approached, key military leaders came to agree with the conclusions of a June 1943 memo by the War Department Strategy Section of the Operations Division: "It is becoming increasingly evident that the State Department advice and assistance during the planning period is not only desirable but necessary."[19] As the problems associated with the end of the war became pressing, military staffers associated with the War Department, Navy Department, and the Joint Chiefs all began to

---

[16] Ibid., 68.
[17] Ibid., 68.
[18] Ibid., 68.
[19] U. S. Army, Center of Military History, *Washington Command Post: The Operations Division*, by Robert Cline, U.S. Government Printing Office. (Washington, DC 1951), 317.

make recommendations for institutional arrangements designed to enhance cooperation with their counterparts in the State Department. Many of these proposals made specific reference to the British War Cabinet as a model for the U.S. to emulate.[20]

From these proposals, the U.S. created a new State-War-Navy Coordinating Committee at the level of assistant secretaries of the three departments. The committee played a critical role over the next two-and-a-half years in facilitating political-military cooperation on such complex issues as the Japanese surrender terms, the occupation of Germany and Japan, U.S. policy toward China, and the management of relations with an increasingly difficult Soviet Union.[21] The Joint Chiefs of Staff, which still had no legislative mandate, had no formal representation on the new committee; but documents produced by the committee relating to military matters were routinely shared with the Joint Chiefs.[22] As the committee became more influential, it also became more of a problem for the Department of State. The State Department representative to the committee was frequently outvoted by the two military services on issues relating to postwar occupation and strategy. This committee skewed American policy towards military solutions to political problems.[23] It also was a significant factor in the formulation of U.S. containment policy and served as a model for the National Security Council.[24] Samuel Huntington summed up civilian military relationship this way: "American civil-military relations in World War II paralleled in some respects those of Germany in World War I...When war came, the American military did not reach out

---

[20] Stuart, *Creating the National Security State*, 69.

[21] Ibid., 117.

[22] Alan Ciamporcero, *The State-War-Navy Coordinating Committee and the Beginning of the Cold War*, PhD. Dissertation, State University of New York at Albany, Graduate School of Public Affairs, 1980, 29.

[23] Ciamporcero, *The State-War-Navy Coordinating Committee and the Beginning of the Cold War*, 43.

[24] Ibid., 88.

after power-Marshall was no Ludendorff. Instead, power was unavoidably thrust upon them."[25]

During the course of World War II, the paradigm that defined civil-military relations shifted. Legally, only the President exercised command of the entire Army and, with the help of the service secretaries, established policies controlling its activities. The Chief of Staff and Chief of Naval Operations were merely the adviser and executive agents of the President and Service Secretaries, and literally the Chief of the War and Navy Department's Staff. However, President Roosevelt and later Truman tended to rely on the Joint Chiefs of Staff and routinely communicated directly with them bypassing the service secretaries, providing increased implied power to these positions. Similar to how the Grant-Lincoln relationship increased the implied power of the Commanding General during the American Civil War.

Army Chief of Staff George Marshall recommended the Joint Chiefs of Staff have a Chief of Staff position within the JCS to perform as the chairman. Marshall envisioned the Chief of Staff would function as a permanent liaison between the Joint Chiefs and the president.[26] Marshall's rationale and purpose was unclear to President Roosevelt. This became evident when Admiral Leahy, Roosevelt's choice for Chairman, became more the Chief of Staff of the president and less the chairman of the Chiefs of Staff.[27] Admiral Leahy became the precursor to the current President's Chief of Staff.

Presidents Roosevelt and Truman sidelined the Department of State during the war. Both of them looked toward military leadership for advice on all aspects of national

[25] Samuel P. Huntington, *The Solider and the State* (Massachusetts: President and fellows of Harvard College, 1957), 316.

[26] Stuart, *Creating the National Security State,* 53.

[27] Ibid.

security matters. This led to a perception that the two military services now had responsibilities for influencing all aspects of national security policy. An internal memo within the Operations Division of the War Department in 1945 reflects this perception, "The time has come when, whether we like it or not, the War Department must face the fact that it has a real interest in political matters of varying categories."[28] The military now perceived itself as a player in setting policy for national diplomacy.

Debates leading up to the 1947 NSA

The debates that led up to passage of the 1947 NSA were arduous and emotional. They could have easily stalled or ended in gridlock, but instead they remained on the forefront of the national agenda because the President of the United States championed this reform. When President Truman was sworn in as the 33rd president he noted in his memoirs: "One of the strongest convictions which I brought to the office of the President was that the antiquated defense setup of the United States had to be reorganized quickly as a step toward insuring our future safety and preserving world peace."[29]

General Marshall made a strong case for unification in the winter of 1943 when he presented a report to the JCS that concluded that "this war is, and future wars undoubtedly will be, largely a series of combined operations in each of which ground, air and sea forces must be employed together and coordinated under one directing hear."[30] The report called for the creation of a single Department of War, headed by a Secretary of War and organized into ground, sea, air, and supply components. It also envisioned a

---

[28] U. S. Army, Center of Military History, *Washington Command Post: The Operations Division*, 331.

[29] Stuart, *Creating the National Security State*, 86.

[30] Ibid., 81.

34

joint general staff arrangement, modeled on the wartime JCS.[31] The Navy was against

such unification and President Roosevelt was unwilling to consider it while the war was

ongoing.

Secretary of the Navy, James Forrestal, led the Navy's attack against unification

of the military as laid out by Marshall. Forrestal's argument was that constitutionally

there could only be one designated Commander in Chief. He also voiced that the Navy

would oppose any scheme that threatened the Marine Corps or naval aviation.[32] Navy

supporters in Congress also questioned the wisdom of any plan to reorganize the military

without addressing the larger issue of reform of the national security structure.

Forrestal looked to a close friend, Ferdinand Eberstadt, to produce a report that

the Navy could use to counter the War Department's unification effort.[33] Eberstadt's

report completed in September of 1945, aligned with Forrestal's main argument against

unification and that the principles of the Constitution were still the centerpiece of logic

against reform. However, Eberstadt's report did support the Air Force as a separate

service and introduced a security council modeled after the British War Cabinet and the

State-War-Navy Coordinating Committee.[34]

The Eberstadt report came at the problem from a different viewpoint that focused

on the national security structure more than the military services. His plan involved

replacing a single defense secretary with the National Security Council with the service

organizations remaining unchanged except for the creation of the Air Force. The

---

[31] Ibid., 81.

[32] Ibid., 84.

[33] Ibid., 88.

[34] Ibid., 89.

Eberstadt report did resonate with both sides of the argument in its premise that the essence of any postwar system should "institutionalize the relationship between those responsible for foreign policy and those responsible for military policy so that the proper balance will be maintained without endangering civilian supremacy."[35]

The final version of the National Security Act of 1947 (NSA) was a compromise from both sides of the military unification debate. Despite the compromises, the Navy and Marine Corps went dragging and kicking into the new National Military Enterprise. Additionally, the NSA implemented changes to the national security structure. The responsibility of developing national security policies prior to 1947 resided with the President. The Chief Executive required both the inclination and ability to formulate such policies himself. The establishment of institutional means and body that could assist the president with weighing individual recommendations of his advisors and judging public opinion on security matters was a significant part of the 1947 NSA with the creation of the National Security Council.

The 1947 NSA was a positive move towards jointness in the military. However, inter-service rivalries continued and the JCS struggled to achieve a national security outlook. This is reflected in Eisenhower's diary in March 1949 after he was asked to preside over JCS meetings as an informal chairman, "The situation grows intolerable. I am so weary of this inter-service struggle for position, prestige and power that this morning I practically blew my top."[36] Eisenhower would take this perception with him when he became President. During his presidency, the JCS's inability to put aside

---

[35] Ibid., 116.

[36] Stephen E. Ambrose, *Eisenhower, Vol I, Soldier, General of the Army, President-Elect: 1890-1952,* (New York: Simon and Schuster, 1983), 487.

service interests and achieve a national outlook continued to disturb him. Eisenhower was unable to achieve any further significant reform in the military or national security organization during his presidency.

Analysis

The United States' position on the global stage evolved tremendously since 1776. In 170 years, the U.S. grew from a fledgling nation fighting for independence to the most powerful nation on the planet. The time period surrounding World War II demonstrated that governmental processes and institutions lagged behind the growing role the U.S. had in the world. Prior to this time, the U.S. could survive with an inefficient security structure. But two world wars and a Cold War on the horizon, made reforming the national security structure and military organizations a necessity and matter of survival, not only for the U.S. but also for the free world.

The 1947 NSA was the first legislation successfully enacted to reform the national security structure since the U.S. Constitution. In order to achieve this level of reform, it required an active role from the highest level of government. President Truman not only recognized the need to reform, but also understood that the status quo was no longer acceptable and became the champion for reform. The debates surrounding military reform spurred the idea to create the National Security Council.

The social environment following the war was such that drastic reforms were possible. In a span of 30 years, the citizens of the United States had endured two world wars with a depression in between. The country was resetting from World War II and realizing that it was now a global power. This new global status required a national security structure capable of leading in the post-World War II era.

Arguably, the U.S. was drawn into World War II regardless of any desire to remain out of the war. However, the way the U.S. entered the war proved to society that current national security structures were inadequate. The U.S. national security structure and military organizations poor performances denied the U.S. the strategic ability to set its desired conditions to enter the War. Instead, Pearl Harbor thrust the U.S. into war.

The lessons from Pearl Harbor highlighted that cooperation between the military departments was ineffective. Additionally, the effectiveness of the temporary organizations established during the war, such as the Joint Chiefs of Staff and the State War Navy Coordinating Committee, provided evidence that new ways of conducting business were not only effective but also possible. This led President Truman and Congress to acknowledge that the lack of a coordinated whole of government approach and/or the status quo of inefficient military organizations to protect national interests would place the country at risk. The U.S. as a global leader required responsible and credible ways and means to lead the world in the post-World War II era.

Achieving change is always hard. However, the debates surrounding change are useful. President Truman's initial effort was to reform the military. During the process of supporting and countering military reform, the need for an organization to assist with developing and coordinating national security policy arose. The idea for a National Security Council spawned from debates over military reform. Reforms implemented by the NSA of 1947 improved but did not resolve many fundamental challenges inhibiting effective joint operations. Significant military operational shortfalls over the next forty years set the stage for the next round of military reform.

CHAPTER 4: GOLDWATER NICHOLS ACT

Chairman of the Joint Chiefs of Staff, Air Force General David C. Jones to a closed session of the House Armed Services Committee on February 3, 1982 in his opening statement stated: "It is not sufficient to have just resources, dollars and weapons systems; we must also have an organization which will allow us to develop the proper strategy, necessary planning, and the full warfighting capability…We do not have an adequate organizational structure today."[1] This was Jones' first formal statement calling for defense organizational reform in the 1980s. The Marine barracks bombing in Beirut, Lebanon and Operation Urgent Fury were another 18 months in the future.

Jones was an advocate for reform early in his tenure as Chairman. Initially, he believed the joint chiefs themselves would reform without external drivers. Eventually, he concurred with Rear Admiral Alfred Thayer Mahan's position that only external forces would result in substantive change by the services toward joint matters.[2] After implementation of the NSA of 1947, multiple presidential commissions documented the Pentagon's continuing problems. Each additional operational military failure served to reinforce the conclusions of previous studies.

Joint Failures

Operation Eagle Claw, a military raid to rescue the American hostages in Iran, suffered from multiple joint planning and execution problems resulting in mission failure on April 25, 1980. Because of maintenance and operators unfamiliarity with onboard

---

[1] James R. Locher, *Victory on the Potomac : The Goldwater-Nichols Act Unifies the Pentagon*, (College Station: Texas A & M University Press, 2002), 34.

[2] Ibid., 43.

systems resulting in pilots returning to the launch point aircraft carrier, only six of eight helicopters arrived at the rendezvous point, "Desert One", with one of the six helicopters unable to continue. This was one short of the minimum required to continue the mission. While at the rendezvous point, a C-130 and helicopter collided, killing five airmen, three marines and destroying both aircraft. The team made a decision to abandon the remaining five helicopters. In doing so, they left behind secret documents, weapons and communications gear creating an embarrassing situation for the U.S. government. The remaining service members boarded the C-130s and returned to their staging areas.

The extreme complexity of the Iranian rescue mission would challenge today's proficient joint special operations organizations. However, in 1980 the joint planning and execution community lacked the planning capability for this type of operation. As a result, the ad hoc planning staff formed blurred lines of authority and responsibility. Strict operational security concerns caused major coordination problems between service components. Compartmented planning efforts provided a fatal flaw; service components had knowledge of their individual actions and not a complete picture of the proposed operation. Because the plan required joint actions, detailed coordination needed for such a complex plan never occurred.

The mission called for helicopters capable of low-level, terrain masking to support nighttime infiltration of the extraction team. The Air Force had qualified pilots, but its helicopters were inadequate for this task. Planners chose Navy RH-53D mine countermeasure helicopters for the operation because the Air Force neglected the requirement to provide helicopters capable of long-range infiltration capability. However, Navy helicopter pilots lacked the training and were not certified in low-level, terrain masking, nighttime flying operations required for this mission. Ultimately, Marine pilots replaced the majority of the Navy pilots because they had low-level certifications.[3]

The lack of a long-range helicopter created a requirement to refuel on the ground before proceeding to extract the hostages. Four Air Force C-130s serving as refuelers met the helicopters at Desert One, the patch in the desert identified as the assembly area. The planned refueling operation was on the ground versus air-to-air refueling.

The lack of clear lines of authority and responsibility existing in the planning manifested itself down to the tactical level. Activities in the assembly area at "Desert One" lacked established command and control procedures and clear lines of communications.[4] The communications equipment at Desert One was incompatible and the plan lacked details to conduct the operations with such limitations. These factors, combined with lack of joint doctrine and training, led to disaster at "Desert One." The events at Desert One epitomized the military's inability to successfully, train, plan for, and execute joint operations. It also highlighted the pentagon's inept acquisition strategy.

On October 23, 1983, in Beirut, Lebanon, a truck loaded with explosives sped past the guard post and blew up the Marine Barracks killing 241, including 220 marines. This was the largest number of marine deaths in a single day since the WORLD WAR II battle of Iwo Jima.[5] The disaster resulted due to the nation's unpreparedness to deal with virulent terrorism.[6] Lebanon was in a quasi-civil war during this time, but DoD was

---

[3] Ibid., 47.

[4] Ibid.

[5] Ibid., 127.

[6] Ibid.

clearly focused on the Cold War and failed to give other missions the appropriate amount of attention.

The disaster placed a spotlight on command relationships within the U.S. European Command, the unified command responsible for the Lebanon mission, and revealed limited authority by the EUCOM commander and dysfunctional barriers imposed by the Navy and Marine chains of command.[7] The principal cause of the bombing did not point to organizational problems, but did involve intelligence shortfalls. The Beirut bombing was another military failure leading to perceptions of inefficient military organizations and this perception reinforced the need for reform. The Beirut bombing resonated deeply with Congressman Bill Nichols of Alabama who was opposed to the U.S. mission in Lebanon and had visited the Marines there one month prior to the bombing.

Two days after the bombing in Beirut, American forces invaded the Caribbean island nation of Grenada. Operation Urgent Fury began at 0500 on October 25, 1983. Grenada's Marxist government, supported by Castro's Marxist Cuban government, was building an airfield capable of handling large military aircraft. The prospect of Libyan and Soviet bloc government planting seeds of revolutionary warfare in Central America concerned President Reagan and the leaders of the island nations of the Antilles.[8] The civilian government of Grenada dissolved after the murder of the country's leader and several cabinet members on October 12, 1983. A Revolutionary Military Council took

---

[7] Ibid.

[8] Office of the Chairman of the Joint Chiefs of Staff, Joint History Office, *Operation Urgent Fury*, by Ronald H. Cole, (Chairman of the Joint Chiefs of Staff. Washington, D.C., 1997), pg 10. http://www.dtic.mil/doctrine/doctrine/history/urgfury.pdf

control and imposed a twenty-four hour curfew.[9] U.S. government officials feared that American citizens trapped in Grenada including medical students were in danger. The President tasked DoD to develop a plan for the evacuation of American citizens.

Operation Urgent Fury while viewed as a success in the public eye, suffered from many joint planning and execution problems. A group of medical students in a third campus-whose rescue was the rationale for the invasion in the first place-went undiscovered for days.[10]

The first few days of the operation saw uncoordinated operations by U.S. Army Rangers and U.S. Marines and the absence of joint air support.[11] The Army and Marine Corps fought side-by-side but with separate chains of command. Lack of interoperable communications exacerbated systemic unity of command. Navy radios could not communicate with Army radio equipment, delaying and complicating requests for naval support. Soldiers requesting supporting fires and in sight of Navy warships, delayed operations waiting for distant Air Force gunships and Army helicopters with compatible radios.[12] Inadequate maps forced ground units to rely on tourist maps. Logistic planning was inadequate, resulting in troops apprehending necessary items from local businesses or homes.[13]

Operation Urgent Fury highlighted inadequate and inefficient processes within DoD. This was primarily a result of the inefficient DoD organization and the lack of

---

[9] Ibid.

[10] Locher, *Victory on the Potomac*, 135.

[11] Office of the Chairman of the Joint Chiefs of Staff, Joint History Office, *Operation Urgent Fury*, 67.

[12] Ibid.

[13] Ibid.

appropriate joint command and control authorities. Service centric acquisition occurred without any consideration of joint interoperability. Joint Doctrine and training were nearly non-existent. Joint command and control proved impossible. The Cold War was nearing its apex and the DoD's ability to support U.S. containment strategy showed signs of weakness. The joint planning and execution deficiencies evident during the Vietnam War became glaring examples as a result of failures during Eagle Claw, the Beirut bombing, and Urgent Fury.[14] The DoD desperately needed a solution to unify command of joint operations and these events became the catalyst for Goldwater-Nichols.

Road to Reform

General Jones' statement to the House Armed Service Committee in 1982 resonated with a staffer who convinced Congressman Richard C. White, the investigations subcommittee chairman, to take up this issue.[15] Congressman White placed JCS reform on the subcommittee agenda and initiated hearings shortly thereafter.

General Jones walked out onto a ledge calling for defense reform. His ideas were not widely supported throughout DoD. The only mutual support Jones had been when Army Chief of Staff Ed Meyer initially supported reform, but succumbed to political pressure and ultimately withdrew his support for reform. Secretary of Defense, Casper Weinberger, and other members of the Joint Chiefs did not agree that the JCS required any type of reform making reform a steep uphill battle. Additionally, the executive branch, led by Secretary Weinberger who was disinterested in DoD reform, sat idly on the sideline.

---

[14] Ibid., 445.

[15] James R. Locher, *Victory on the Potomac*, 62.

Congressman Newt Gingrich provided testimony at the first hearing stating, "The central problems of American survival are not budget, resource, or hardware problems. The real threats to our ability to survive are intellectual and organizational…and the current system is not working. Historically countries reform their military only after major defeats…[Congress should] spend more time thinking about defense, because we desperately need reform without defeat."[16]

Congressman White sponsored the "Joint Chiefs of Staff Reorganization Act of 1982" which won approval in the House of Representatives. However, the Act fell well short of the reforms General Jones had called for and died in the Senate and failed to become law. Congressman White retired and when the Ninety-Eighth Congress convened in January 1983, Congressman Bill Nichols of Alabama decided to chair the Investigations Subcommittee of the House Armed Services Committee.[17]

Congressman Nichols kept JCS reform on the docket and asked Secretary Weinberger for his response to the previous reform bill passed by the House. Secretary Weinberger summed up his thoughts in February 1983 to Congressman Nichols by saying, "the JCS system is already working well…Good people are what it takes to make the JCS system work."[18] This clearly demonstrated Weinberger's position that authorities and processes were not important, but individuals who could "get along" were. The subcommittee held a variety of hearings and, on October 17, 1983, the House passed H.R. 3718. This bill made limited structural changes to the JCS and expanded the authority of the Chairman of the JCS as a formal member of the National Security

---

[16] Ibid., 68.

[17] Ibid., 94.

[18] Ibid., 100.

Council. The bill also expanded the responsibilities, size, and authorities of the joint staff to assist the chairman in carrying out his responsibilities.[19] Congressman Nichols always viewed JCS reform as a left over from White, but that changed six days later with the bombing of the Marine barracks in Beirut.[20]

After the Beirut bombing, Nichols, who opposed to the U.S. mission in Lebanon, led the House of Representatives investigation to determine the cause. Nichols held multiple hearings and inquiries into the bombing, concluding that not only did the JCS require reform, but also the authority and capacity of unified commanders were out of balance with the responsibility and accountability expected of them.[21] Nichols' subcommittee drafted legislation to remedy the problems. However, Senator Tower, Chairman of the Senate Armed Services Committee (SASC), not interested in reform, engaged in legislative maneuvering to keep the House bill off the Senate floor.[22]

The situation changed when Senator Tower retired from the Senate in November 1984 and Senator Barry Goldwater became the new chairman of the SASC. Goldwater, an Air Force reservist, made defense reorganization his number one priority.[23] The House agreed on DoD reform and sent their proposed bill the Senate. Senator Goldwater interpreted the battle lines in the Senate and it took some time for the Senate to form their opinions on reform.

---

[19] Ibid., 111.

[20] Ibid., 112.

[21] Ibid., 157.

[22] Ibid, 186. Mr. Locher infers that Sen Tower, a navy reservist, aligns with the predominte Navy and OSD opinion that reform is not necessary. He describes in Chapter 9 the environment surrounding the reform and Sen Tower's position by stating that "Tower had adroitly found reasons to put off JCS reorganization without having to declare his opposition."

[23] Ibid., 213.

Goldwater, a Republican, had the support of the SASC ranking member, Senator Nunn, a Democrat, provided reform leadership representation from both parties. Goldwater's reorganization effort picked up where President Eisenhower left off twenty-eight years earlier with some problems tracing back as far as the Spanish-American War.[24]

Eisenhower, throughout his presidency, was concerned that rivalry between military organizations clouded the personal judgment of senior officers. Additionally, Eisenhower believed that the 1947 and 1949 NSAs did not increase unity of command. In reference to the 1947 NSA President Eisenhower said, "the lessons [of WORLD WAR II] were lost, tradition won…the need for unity is most acute at two points-OSD and COCOMs [who are] responsible for actual combat."[25]

Senators Goldwater and Nunn recognized the significance of DOD reform and understood the necessity for strategic legislative maneuvering to prevent opponents from killing or stalling their reform efforts. The Department of the Navy continued to voice opposition over any type of reform throughout the process and strived to gain congressional support for their antireform views. The executive branch remained largely quiet on the subject, but Secretary Weinberger's position was any reform should be via executive direction, not congressional legislation. Over the next 18 months, Goldwater and Nunn strategically and methodically navigated DOD reform through the Armed Services Committee culminating on May 7, 1986 when the Barry Goldwater Department

---

[24] Ibid., 351.

[25] David Jablonsky, "Eisenhower and the Origins of Unified Command." *Joint Force Quarterly : JFQ*, no. 23 (Autumn 1999/2000, 1999): 24-31, http://search.proquest.com/docview/203628017?accountid=12686.

of Defense Reorganization Act of 1986 passed a full Senate vote by 95-0 in favor of DOD reorganization.[26]

Meanwhile, the House of Representatives, who initiated DOD reform years earlier following General Jones' testimony in 1982, had a much more narrow view of reform than the Goldwater Nunn efforts in the Senate. The House of Representatives already demonstrated support for JCS reform, but now needed to expand its scope of reform to include unified command. The House Armed Service Committee agreed to investigate similar reforms to those addressed by the Senate. Congressman Nichols led the effort and on August 5, 1986 passed an amendment to the already approved DOD reform bill to include unified command reform. The house vote was 406-4. Only four of over 500 voting members of Congress opposed the legislation, demonstrating both houses of Congress overwhelmingly supported DOD reform.

The House and Senate versions of the bill after final committee markup was named for the bill's Chairman Senator Goldwater and Vice Chairman Congressman Nichols and renamed it the Goldwater Nichols Department of Defense Act of 1986.[27] The Goldwater Nichols Act passed a voice vote in the Senate and House on September 16th & 17th respectively and submitted for President's signature on September 19.[28] With overwhelming support in Congress, a Presidential veto was unlikely. President Reagan waited until the last possible moment and signed the Goldwater Nichols Act without any fanfare.[29]

---

[26] Locher, *Victory on the Potomac*, 421.

[27] Ibid., 426.

[28] Ibid., 430.

[29] Ibid., 433.

Congress declared nine purposes for the Goldwater Nichols Act: 1) strengthen civilian authority; 2) improve military advice; 3) place clear responsibility on combatant commanders for accomplishment of assigned missions; 4) ensure that the authority of combatant commanders is commensurate with their responsibility; 5) increase attention to strategy formulation and contingency planning; 6) provide for the more efficient use of resources; 7) improve joint officer management; 8) enhance the effectiveness of military operations; and 9) improve DOD management.[30] James Locher III, architect of the Goldwater Nichols Act, summed up the effort: "The Goldwater Nichols Act completed the reorganization efforts started eighty-five years earlier in the aftermath of the Spanish-American War. It finally corrected the distortions of power and influence that emerged during World War II [that] had troubled U.S. security for forty years thereafter."[31]

Analysis

The Goldwater Nichols Act of 1986 cemented Eisenhower's idea of unified command and institutionalized joint into DoD. It became the driving force that completed DoD's evolution from coordination to integration for the planning and execution of joint operations. Also, the global environment began its shift from bi-polar to a multi-polar world and the Goldwater Nichols Act assisted in this transition by addressing the inadequate level of jointness within DoD. DoD proved it could not reform itself and Congress became the external force to impart change within the military structure. Personalities played a critical role in the successful passage of this legislation.

---

[30] Congress, House. *Goldwater-Nichols Department of Defense Reorganization Act of 1986: Conference Report [To accompany H.R. 3622].* 99th Congress, 2d session. Report 99-824, section 3.

[31] Locher, *Victory on the Potomac*, 436.

The U.S. and the United Soviet Socialist Republic (USSR) opposed each other over the diametrically opposed philosophies of Democracy and Communism. The U.S. as the leader of the free world internalized the responsibility to promote democratic ideals throughout the world while containing the spread of Communism. The U.S. Military, a prominent instrument of power for protecting U.S. national interests and democratic way of life in the world, increasingly found itself engaged in regional crisis unrelated to the containment of Communism. The Soviet Union maintained a façade of strength reinforcing the perception of a bi-polar world even though signals of weakness began to show themselves in the early 1980s. U.S. operations in Lebanon and six years later in Iraq reflect this paradigm shift away from a bi-polar world and towards a world in which economies and security became more globally interrelated. With the rise of bi-polar influences, regional security became increasingly more important to protecting U.S. national interests against non-traditional threats. The Goldwater Nichols Act was pivotal to ensure DoD become increasingly more unified and flexible enough to respond to the diverse nature of threats in a multi-polar world.

Numerous U.S. military operations after World War II provided evidence that the security structure within the DoD was not efficient or effective for joint operations. Korea, Vietnam, Iranian Hostage Rescue, the Beirut bombing, and invasion of Grenada demonstrated that the U.S. military structure and processes had weaknesses. Military failures shared several characteristics: poor military advice to civilian leadership, lack of unity of command, and inability of services to operate effectively in a joint environment.[32] Additionally, mismanaged acquisition strategies and perceptions of wasteful spending fed public opinion necessitating military reform.[33]

After General Jones' statement to the House Armed Service Committee in 1982 calling for reform, it took over four years to gain sufficient support in Congress to pass the Goldwater-Nichols Act. Overarching and comprehensive legislative reform of executive branch functions is difficult to accomplish because of the checks and balance framework established by the founding fathers in the U.S. Constitution. The road to passage of the Goldwater Nichols Act highlights the significant roles personalities play in the outcome of reform efforts.

Change is always difficult and recognizing when to institutionalize change is just as important as the change itself. General Jones recognized that DoD required a level of change. He also understood that DoD was unable to achieve the depth of transformation he desired on its own and it would take action by a superior organization with responsibilities and authorities over DoD, that being Congress. DoD leadership, specifically Secretary Weinberger, did not agree with General Jones and his reform desires. General Jones took a calculated risk using the House Armed Service Committee hearing to voice his concerns. Congressional representatives White and Nichols effectively navigated limited reform legislation through the House of Representatives. The real fight was in the Senate, where broad overarching reform debates took place.

---

[32] James R. Locher III, "Has is worked? The Goldwater-Nichols Reorganization Act," *Naval War College Review, 54* (Autumn 2001), pg 99.

[33] Robert P. Kozloski, "Building the Purple Ford." *Naval War College Review* 65, no. 4 (09, 2012): pg 44, http://ezproxy6.ndu.edu/login?url=http://search.ebscohost.com/login.aspx?direct=true&db=aph&AN=7920 0721&site=ehost-live&scope=site.

Senator Tower, who opposed military reform, used his position as chairman of the Senate Armed Services Committee to stall any reform efforts. His position as chairman allowed him to set the committee agenda, resulting in military reform being placed so far down the agenda that the committee never debated it under his leadership. The timing of his retirement and Senator Goldwater's selection to replace him was pivotal to the success of military reform. The environment and societal norms during the early 1980s were such that military reform was acceptable, but reform success still required action from proponents to champion it. The additional support of the ranking member, Senator Sam Nunn, solidified the bi-partisan effort needed to pass overarching and comprehensive legislative reform of the military.

Similar to the 1947 NSA, Goldwater-Nichols reform encompassed elements of the entire military organization, something Secretary Root was unable to achieve in 1903. The difference between the depth and span of reform after the Spanish-American War compared to 1947 NSA and Goldwater-Nichols is the level at which the reform was championed. Substantive reform requires political fortitude and possessing a level of authority over all aspects of desired reform. President Truman made it his personal agenda to accomplish reform post WORLD WAR II and Congress led the Goldwater-Nichols effort. Both of these successful efforts in achieving broad reform were a result of the champion being at the appropriate level reflective of the breadth of desired reform.

The military weaknesses that Goldwater Nichols addressed were the same weaknesses in the national security structure that were slowly coming into light. The shift towards a dynamic multi-polar world with ambiguous threats challenged the capabilities of the U.S. national security structure to properly address them. This structure increasingly became incapable of synchronizing efforts across all instruments of national power. The fall of the USSR delayed this recognition until the small radical organization Al Qaeda attacked the U.S. in a dramatic way on September 11, 2001. This event and the wars that followed in Iraq and Afghanistan, forced the U.S. to relook at its national security structure and identify the reforms required to thrive in the twenty first century.

CHAPTER 5: ANALYSIS AND RECOMMENDATIONS

The U.S. military and national security context during the late nineteenth and early twentieth centuries is similar to today. The Spanish-American War, considered by some as a victory for the U.S., revealed many areas within the national security structure that lacked an efficient organizational construct to support the President with national security challenges including military specific issues in the need of reform and improvement. The lack of an external reform champion and the overriding political philosophy of "why change a good thing" prevented real reform or improvements from taking place. Today, after a decade of continuous war, the U.S. is out of Iraq and postured to leave Afghanistan by the end of 2014. Iraq and Afghanistan will likely end up in the modest win column for the U.S.; but like the lessons from the Spanish-American War, there are currently many areas in need of improvement and reform in the military and national security structure.

The current political environment dominated by bipartisan politics is not ripe for the emergence of a political entity willing to take on the role of external reform champion. Therefore, if any reform efforts are to be undertaken, DoD is the most likely candidate to become an internal reform champion for the national security structure. First, DoD must find a way to maintain the level of jointness it has achieved over the last decade of combat operations. Second, DoD must lead change within the national security structure by leading and exemplifying transformational change within itself. Change within the U.S. National Security organization never occurs by happenstance and identifying and implementing the necessary changes will be difficult.

Personalities matter, and the depth and breadth of reform as demonstrated by historic examples depend on the individual championing it. Substantive changes requires dedicated individuals with audacity, strategic vision, and necessary authorities to direct changes and champion the cause through the strategic political juggernaut that defines the U.S. government process. Secretary Root, President Truman and Senator Goldwater possessed these qualities and were able to achieve significant reform of the military and national security structure. However, the genesis of reform generally begins at echelons below those who lead change at the political level.

Planting the seeds of reform is just as important as growing them. This requires subordinates with access to the individual(s) who champion change at the strategic political level. Seeds of reform come in many different forms. Schofield demonstrated his beliefs by the way he executed his responsibilities as commanding general and Upton documented his on organizational changes required in the War Department. Schofield and Upton played just as an important role to reform, as did Secretary Elijhi Root in achieving it after the Spanish-American War. While Schofield and Upton lacked the authority for the depth and breadth of their desired changes, they possessed the strategic vision and audacity to plant the seeds of reform until Root, someone with the authority, could nurture them to fruition in concert with societal norms.

General Jones recognizing that DoD reform required external pressures, pleaded his case to the HASC in the hope that a Congressman would latch on to his ideas. His testimony resonated with Congressman White who passed the torch to Congressman Nichols. Personalities in the Senate blocked early House of Representatives DoD reform efforts and it was not until Senator Goldwater became SASC chairman, did reform become a potential reality.

Comprehensive reform requires time to gestate within the political environment before it can come to fruition. The time required depends upon the social environment and timing of the strategic catalyst to spur debates. Upton and Schofield presented their ideas twenty years before implementation when fallout from the Spanish-American War provided the catalyst to enact their reform ideas. Truman recognized the need for military reform as a Senator investigating the shortfalls into the successful attack on Pearl Harbor by the Japanese. Six years and Truman's rise to the presidency, in conjunction with the post World War II environment, combined to set the social and political conditions allowing passage of the 1947 NSA. General Jones' testimony occurred four years before passage of Goldwater Nichols. The height of the Cold War and several military operations failure to demonstrate jointness provided the environment and catalyst to instill joint into the DoD lexicon.

Organizations tend to resist change and usually require an external force to implement it. Achieving lasting reform in the DoD or the national security structure requires legislation as the external force to cement it into law. Reform is always framed by the environment and societal norms of the time. Mark Stoler, author of *General Marshall, Solider-Statesman of the Twenty First Century*, in detailing the creation of formal military staffs, describes how societal norms set conditions for reform, and establish the environment requiring military organizations reflect the society it represents.

> The advent of staffs and armies in the late nineteenth century was far from accidental, for they represented the application of the principles of mass production and scientific management from the industrial revolution to the armed forces. The industrial revolution provided not merely new implements of war. It

also provided the material capacity, the professional expertise, and the organizational ability to feed, clothe, arm, train, and rapidly move huge numbers of men. In effect, the armed forces of Europe were experiencing the same technological and managerial revolutions that were affecting society as a whole.[1]

Major changes in government organizations are often achieved following major combat operations or in response to viable existential threat. These conditions involving war or threats to security, take place within the context of society and its norms. Before the Spanish-American War and the joint military failures in the early 1980s, the mindset of "why change" prevailed. Following the Spanish-American War, there was not an existential threat and therefore the breadth of reform was limited to the War Department.

The Japanese attack on Pearl Harbor demonstrated that the U.S. military structure was incapable of executing its national responsibilities successfully. World War II enlightened and provided experiences for senior military and political members into a different more efficient military organizational construct. Additionally, following World War II and the joint military failures in the early 1980s, communism, an existential threat was present. These conditions, in concert with a political champion, enabled overarching and comprehensive reform to take place.

As DoD begins to withdraw out of Afghanistan after over a decade of combat operations, society is ripe to accept changes to U.S. government organizations. The fiscal environment presents future challenges, driving the need to find efficient ways to maintain the level of jointness achieved over the last decade. Former Secretary of Defense, Leon Panetta, told Congress how devastating a hollow force is to our national security. DoD is downsizing and Americans expect their military to maintain its

---

[1] Mark A. Stoler, *George C. Marshall: Solider-Statesman of the American Century* (New York: Simon & Schuster Macmillan, 1989), 20.

influence by remaining strong and efficient. As the force gets smaller, a proficient, integrated force well versed in joint operations will help ensure the U.S. military remains dominate long into the twenty first century.

The current military force joint proficiency is a result from a decade of joint employment in combat operations. Joint operations require extensive coordination and the only way to be good at joint is practice and operating in a joint context. The lack of joint opportunities allows the services to revert to service specific core capabilities often executed in a singular domain. The six joint functions designed to help the joint force commander to integrate, synchronize and direct operations are most effective when employed across all warfighting domains. The last decade has provided endless joint opportunities executed routinely in operations in Iraq and Afghanistan. As the U.S. draws down from operations in Afghanistan, it must now find a way to maintain joint proficiency in routine training exercises amplifying the cross service integration of the six joint functions.

Shrinking budgets require tradeoffs on how to best use limited training dollars to maintain joint proficiency. The military services must evaluate where to take risk between building service competencies and maintaining jointness through exercises. This is both a service and a joint problem. However, the current budget system places the burden of funding most joint training on the backs of the services. The Joint Chiefs of Staff (JCS), comprised of the service chiefs along with the chairman of the JCS, must maintain joint military proficiency. Nevertheless, the service chiefs are often unable to divorce themselves from their service equities. The debates surrounding the 1947 NSA and Goldwater Nichols Act demonstrate that the parochialism is how services respond to shrinking budgets. Decisions affecting joint proficiency require action before inter-service rivalries create an atmosphere of parochialism as services justify their share of a shrinking budget.

DoD's planning, programming, budgeting, and execution system is not optimized for joint equities. PPBE system evolved over time to give combatant commanders greater input into the programming and budgeting process. The roots of PPBE go back to Defense Secretary McNamara in the 1960s and are long overdue for modernization. As long as the bulk of the budget responsibilities remain with the services and the JCS is comprised of sitting service chiefs, maintaining joint proficiency will give way to service competencies.

History demonstrates that DoD reform is the leading indicator for reform of the national security structure. Deconfliction, coordination, and integration describe the stages of military evolution. Prior to the 1890s, the military primarily deconflicted operations between the services. With the Spanish-American War, the U.S. military began the transition from deconfliction to coordination. It took World War II and another forty years, for the military to encapsulate coordination in all major aspects of operations. Following WORLD WAR II and the NSA 1947, the transition to integration began. It took over forty years and additional legislation, 1986 Goldwater Nichols Act, for joint to evolve within all DoD activities (operations plus organize, train and equip). It is now time for the national security structure to follow.

The national security structure established by the U.S. Constitution had elements of coordination, but the elements of national power primarily operated independently. Not until the NSC created in 1947 did the national security structure have any sufficient means to coordinate efforts between instruments of national power. The national security structure has not reformed since 1947 and today uses the framework established for a post World War II era. The Project for National Security Reform (PNSR), chartered by the 2008 National Defense Authorization Act (NDAA), identified five critical problems in the national security structure[2]. To date, the five problems still exist and the current administration is not exercising any efforts to solve them. The political leadership is distracted with partisan politics and is unable to prioritize even what the federal government needs to fund. Complex twenty first century challenges do not allow the U.S. national security structure the luxury of another one hundred fifty years to evolve to an integrated whole of government approach if it plans to thrive in this multi-polar world.

The global environment is changing at a break neck pace. Time and space are luxuries that no longer exist. Each year, the world becomes more interconnected. Additionally, security threats no longer require an army to achieve effects, nor are threats predominately perpetrated by nation states. The click of a mouse can produce effects that once required an explosive device to accomplish. The emergence of the cyber domain and the information revolution gives non-traditional threats access to capabilities previously out of reach due to time, distance, cost complexity, and limited resources. Radical groups have access to millions of people and endless information streams to pursue their agendas. Nation states still dominate, but today's threats remain ambiguous and cover a wide spectrum. This dynamic environment sets conditions where power can be distributed globally and global leadership provided outside the traditional nation state model. For instance, the European Union could be the global diplomatic power with its

---

[2] Project on National Security Refrom (PNSR), *Forging a New Shield*, (Washington DC: PNSR, November 2008), vi.

ability to create coalitions, the U.S. the global information power, and China the global military and economic power. The twenty first century framed by the information age and globalization sets the stage for a multidimensional global power struggle in which the U.S. national security structure is ill suited.

The national security structure established in 1947 was for a bi-polar world to counter a similar foe, the United Soviet Socialist Republic. The National Security Council proved to be a critical strategic enabler assisting U.S. leadership with their leading global role. The post-World War II era national security focused on nuclear deterrence and major combat operations. Vertical pillars of excellence grew within the government and only required limited coordination to counter successfully the Cold War threat. The NSC came into being as an offshoot from debates surrounding military reform post World War II. The National Security Council functions were never the focus of reform.

Designing an organizational structure to enable integrated approaches was never considered. Since the NSA 1947, each major national security reform has been piecemeal, focusing on individual system components (e.g., DOD, Intelligence Community, and Department of Homeland Security) and not on the national security system as a whole.[3] As a result, the U.S. has vertical pillars of expertise trying to solve horizontal global problems.

Secretary of War, Elihu Root described the military departments in 1902 in a report to Congress by stating:

---

[3] Project on National Security Refrom (PNSR), *Turning Ideas into Action*, (Washington DC: PNSR, September 2009), 14.

Our military system is…exceedingly defective at the top…We have the different branches of the military service well organized, each within itself, for the performance of its duties. But when we come to the coordination and direction of all these means and agencies of warfare, so that all parts of the machine shall work true together, we are weak. Our system makes no adequate provision for the directing brain, which every army must have to work successfully.[4]

Secretary Root's statement over one hundred years ago resonates today describing the national security structure by replacing military system with National Security Staff, military service with government, and army with agency. The basic deficiency of the current system is that parochial departmental and agency interests, reinforced by Congress, paralyze the interagency cooperation even as the variety, speed, and complexity of emerging security issues prevent the White House from effectively controlling the system.[5]

The U.S. requires a system to bring coherence to understand and respond to complex twenty first century challenges. Individual departments and agencies of the federal government cannot effectively navigate today's complex challenges to develop sound strategies that protect U.S. national interest. The numerous bureaucracies involved in U.S. national security today operate through the lens of their own organizational culture.[6] There is no common national government culture that facilitates the development of common national objectives and a shared vision.[7]

The period of time for the U.S. government to respond to a deficiency within the national security structure is lengthy. The U.S. military structure established by the

---

[4] War Department, *Annual Reports of the War Department for the Fiscal Year Ended June 30, 1902* (Washington DC: Government Printing Office, 190) 42-43.

[5] Roger Z. George and Harvey Rishikof, *The National Security Enterprise; Navigating the Labyrinth*, (Washington, DC: Georgetown University Press, 2011), 2.

[6] Locher III, James R. "THE MOST IMPORTANT THING: Legislative Reform of the National Security System." *Military Review* (Jun2008, 2008): 19-27.

[7] Ibid.

Constitution in 1787 and framed by the 2d Continental Congress in 1775 remained relatively unchanged until the NSA of 1947. Forty-five years earlier, Secretary Root's report to Congress addressed the reforms that the NSA of 1947 finally addressed. It would take another forty years to realize the shortcoming of the NSA of 1947 and reform the military again with the Goldwater-Nichols Act. The Project for National Security Reform completed their report on reform of the national security structure in 2008 identifying critical shortfalls and recommending significant changes to the national security structure. In today's rapidly changing multi-polar world, the U.S. national security structure cannot afford to mirror defense and wait forty-five years to enact national security reform.

Just as Goldwater Nichols shifted power from military services to officials responsible for coordinating them, the U.S. government is in need of the same type of legislation to allow an integrated whole-of-government approach. This type of approach achieves what Secretary Root wanted for the services in 1902: "It makes intelligent command possible by procuring and arranging information and working out plans in detail, and it makes intelligent and effective execution of commands possible by keeping all the separate agents advised of the parts they are to play in the general scheme."[8]

The current environment lacks the political champion like Secretary Root in 1903, President Truman in 1947, and Senator Goldwater and Congressman Nichols in 1986 to navigate reform through the U.S. political landscape in order to legislate necessary reform measures. The President and Congress have abdicated their responsibility to assist in helping DoD decide what is important and therefore needs to be funded. Recent

---

[8] War Department, *Annual Reports of the War Department for the Fiscal Year Ended June 30, 1902,* 46.

increased bipartisan politics pollute the waters even more creating a strategic environment that is unable to address necessary changes in the national security structure.

Ingenuity is what defined America in the ninetieth and twentieth centuries and still does so today: "As it did in the Civil War and …again in World Wars I & II, [Iraq and Afghanistan], the U.S… responded to crisis with improvisation, trial and error, followed by a growing mastery of the circumstances that confronted it."[9] The question now is how long can the U.S. continue to rely on ingenuity to maintain our leading role in the world? The ability to reform the national security structure, increase interagency integration and maintain jointness within the increasingly hostile political and fiscal environment present today will determine how the U.S. plans to meet the challenges of the twenty first century security environment and maintain its position as a world leader.

DoD has led transformation in the national security structure throughout history by reforming itself first. Until the political and social environment is ripe to accept the necessary changes in the national security structure needed today, DoD must continue to demonstrate jointness and improve interagency coordination providing an example for the national security structure to follow. A champion of national security structure reform needs to emerge before twenty first century challenges erode the ability of the U.S. to remain a global super power. It begins with the DoD and its appetite to lead and influence national security reform.

---

[9] Graham Cosmas, *An Army for Empire; the U.S. Army in the Spanish-American War*, (Columbia: University of Missouri Press, 1971), 313.

BIBLIOGRAPHY

Ambrose, Stephen E., *Eisenhower, Vol I, Soldier, General of the Army, President-Elect: 1890-1952*. New York: Simon and Schuster, 1983.

Carlson, Adolf. *Joint U.S. Army-Navy War Planning on the Eve of the First World War: Its Origins and its Legacy*. Carlisle Barracks, PA: Strategic Studies Institute, February 16, 1998.

Ciamporcero, Alan. *The State-War-Navy Coordinating Committee and the Beginning of the Cold War*. PhD. Dissertation. State University of New York at Albany, Graduate School of Public Affairs, 1980.

Congress, House. *Goldwater-Nichols Department of Defense Reorganization Act of 1986: Conference Report [To accompany H.R. 3622]*. 99th Congress, 2d session. Report 99-824, section 3.

Congressional Medal of Honor Society. "Recipients." Congressional Medal of Honor Society. http://www.cmohs.org/recipient-detail/1198/schofield-john-m.php (accessed 20 December 2012).

Cosmas, Graham A. *An Army for Empire; the U.S. Army in the Spanish-American War*. Columbia: University of Missouri Press, 1971.

Cosmas, Graham A., Jack Shulimson, David A. Armstrong, and U.S.. Office of the Chairman of the Joint Chiefs of Staff. Joint History Office. *The Joint Chiefs of Staff and the War in Vietnam, 1960-1968*. Washington, DC: Office of Joint History, Office of the Chairman of the Joint Chiefs of Staff, 2009.

Department of State, Office of the Historian. "Milestones 1801-1829: Monroe Doctrine, 1823." Department of State. http://history.state.gov/milestones/1801-1829/Monroe (accessed November 10, 2012).

Department of State, Office of the Historian. "Biographies of the Secretaries of State: Elihu Root." Department of State. http://history.state.gov/departmenthistory/people/root-elihu (accessed December 31, 2012).

Gaddis, John Lewis. *Surprise, Security and the American Experience*. Cambridge, Massachusetts: President and fellows of Harvard College, 2004.

George, Roger Z. and Rishikof, Harvey. *The National Security Enterprise; Navigating the Labyrinth*. Washington, DC: Georgetown University Press, 2011.

History of the Joint Chiefs of Staff: The Joint Chiefs of Staff and National Policy.
Washington: Office of Joint History Office of the Chairman of the Joint Chiefs of Staff, 1996.

Holwitt, Joel I. "War by Land, Sea and Air: Dwight Eisenhower and the Concept of Unified Command." *U.S. Naval Institute.Proceedings* 136, no. 11 (Nov 2010, 2010): 65, http://search.proquest.com/docview/807440622?accountid=12686.

Huntington, Samuel P. *The Solider and the State.* Cambridge, Massachusetts: President and fellows of Harvard College, 1957.

Jablonsky, David. "Eisenhower and the Origins of Unified Command." *Joint Force Quarterly : JFQ*, no. 23 (Autumn 1999/2000, 1999): 24-31, http://search.proquest.com/docview/203628017?accountid=12686.

Joint Chiefs of Staff. Historical Division. *Origin of the Joint and Combined Chiefs of Staff, Volume I*, Vernon E. Davis. Joint Secretariat. Washington DC, 1972.

Kozloski, Robert P. "Building the Purple Ford." *Naval War College Review* 65, no. 4 (09, 2012): 41-63, http://ezproxy6.ndu.edu/login?url=http://search.ebscohost.com/login.aspx?direct=true&db=aph&AN=79200721&site=ehost-live&scope=site.

Locher III, James R. "Has is worked? The Goldwater-Nichols Reorganization Act." *Naval War College Review 54* (Autumn 2001): 96-99.

Locher III, James R. "THE MOST IMPORTANT THING: Legislative Reform of the National Security System." *Military Review* (Jun2008, 2008): 19-27, http://ezproxy6.ndu.edu/login?url=http://search.ebscohost.com/login.aspx?direct=true&db=aph&AN=63025161&site=ehost-live&scope=site.

Locher III, James R. *Victory on the Potomac : The Goldwater-Nichols Act Unifies the Pentagon.* College Station: Texas A & M University Press, 2002.

Newsmax. "McCain, Graham to Newsmax: Sequestration Will Cause 'Inability to Defend Nation." Newsmax. http://www.newsmax.com/Headline/mccain-graham-sequestration-defense/2012/08/02/id/447451 (accessed December 3, 2012).

New York Times. "On This Day." New York Times on the Web. http://www.nytimes.com/learning/general/onthisday/20100814.html (accessed December 6, 2012).

Office of the Assistant Secretary of Defense (Public Affairs). "News Transcript: DOD News Briefing with Secretary Panetta and Gen. Dempsey from the Pentagon, November 10, 2011." U.S. DoD.

http://www.defense.gov/transcripts/transcript.aspx?transcriptid=4925 (accessed December 3, 2012).

Office of the Chairman of the Joint Chiefs of Staff. Joint History Office. *Operation Urgent Fury*, by Ronald H. Cole. Chairman of the Joint Chiefs of Staff. Washington, D.C., 1997. http://www.dtic.mil/doctrine/doctrine/history/urgfury.pdf

Owens, Mackubin Thomas. "Declining Defense Budgets and the End of 'Jointness'." *National Review on Line.* July 27, 2012. http://www.nationalreview.com/articles/312312/declining-defense-budgets-and-end-jointness-mackubin-thomas-owens# (accessed October 10, 2012).

Phillips, Peter C. and Charles S. Corcoran. "Harnessing America's Power." *JFQ: Joint Force Quarterly*, no. 63 (2011, 2011): 38-46, http://ezproxy6.ndu.edu/login?url=http://search.ebscohost.com/login.aspx?direct=true&db=aph&AN=69635860&site=ehost-live&scope=site.

Project on National Security Refrom (PNSR). *Forging a New Shield.* Washington DC: PNSR, November 2008.

Project on National Security Refrom (PNSR). *Turning Ideas into Action.* Washington DC: PNSR, September 2009.

Schofield, John McAllister. *Forty-Six Years in the Army.* New York, The Century Company, 1897.

Smith, Paul. *Government and the Armed Forces in Britain, 1856-1990.* London, GBR: Continuum International Publishing, 1996. http://site.ebrary.com/lib/nationaldefense/Doc?id=10404949&ppg=173

Stoler, Mark A. George C. Marshall: Solider-Statesman of the American Century. New York: Simon & Schuster Macmillan, 1989.

Stuart, Douglas T. *Creating the National Security State.* New Jersey: Princeton University Press, 2008.

Sydney J. Freedberg Jr. "On 237th Birthday, Navy Feels Its Time Has Come; Budget Pressures Belie Campaign Rhetoric." AOL Defense. http://defense.aol.com/2012/10/09/on-237th-birthday-navy-feels-its-time-has-come-budget-pressure/ (accessed December 3, 2012)

U.S. Air Force, Air University. *Unification of the Armed Forces: Administrative and Legislative Developments 1945-1949,* by R. Earl. McClendon. Documentary Research Division, Research Studies Institute. Maxwell Air Force Base, Alabama, 1952.

U. S. Army. Center of Military History. *Washington Command Post: The Operations Division,* by Robert Cline. U.S. Government Printing Office. Washington, DC (1951).

U.S. Joint Chiefs of Staff. *Doctrine for the Armed Forces of the U.S..* Joint Publication 1. Washington DC; Joint Chiefs of Staff, Incorporating Change 1 March 20, 2009.

U.S. Senate Committee on the Budget. "Charts." Republicans. http://budget.senate.gov/republican/public/index.cfm/charts (accessed December 3, 2012)

War Department. *Annual Reports of the War Department for the Fiscal Year Ended June 30, 1902.* Washington DC: Government Printing Office, 1903.